ROOTS TO THE EARTH

ROOTS TO THE EARTH

BY

WENDELL BERRY

WOOD ENGRAVINGS BY

WESLEY BATES

COUNTERPOINT · BERKELEY

Published by Counterpoint in 2016

Library of Congress Cataloging-in-Publivation Data is Available

This book was handset in Cloister Lightface type cast by Theo Rehak at the Dale Guild. The text was printed on a hand-fed Chandler & Price and the engravings were printed from the wood by the artist on a Vandercook, for reproduction for this trade edition.

Design and composition by Wesley Bates, Leslie Shane, Carolyn Whitesel, and Gray Zeitz at Larkspur Press

ISBN 978-1-61902-780-0

COUNTERPOINT
2560 Ninth Street, Suite 318
Berkeley, CA 94710
www.counterpointpress.com

Printed in Canada
Distributed by Publishers Group West

10 9 8 7 6 5 4 3 2 1

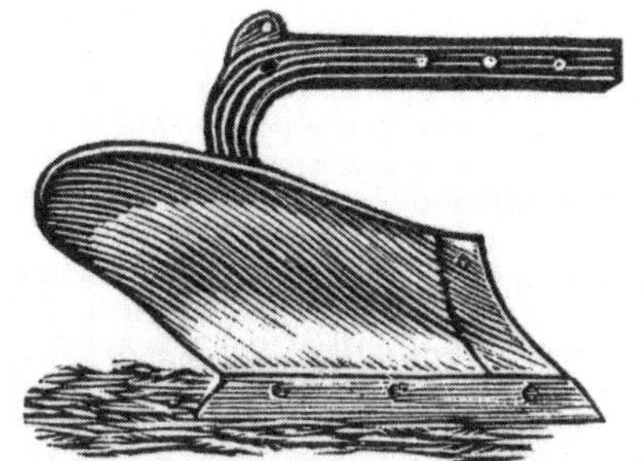

INTRODUCTION

Wendell Berry is a farmer and writer. He lives with his family by the Kentucky River, where he has farmed for nearly fifty years, and has written about as many books of poetry, essays, and fiction.

Wendell Berry writes about culture, agriculture, place, community, love, and life from a deep understanding of his own place. As our society moves toward urbanization, the majority of the population views agriculture from an increasingly detached position. Economic, social, and political pressures on the rural community are becoming more intense. Farming is the most essential of human activities and its vitality is of utmost importance to us and to future generations.

In his poetry Wendell Berry reaches out to what is beautiful and mysterious. He reveals tenderness and love as well as anger and uncertainty. Through his words, one discovers a man with strong convictions and respect for life.

The wood engravings in this collection are intended to be companion pieces to Mr. Berry's words. I have chosen these poems for the way he expresses what it is to be a farmer.

—*Wesley W. Bates*

THE MAN BORN TO FARMING

The grower of trees, the gardener, the man born to farming,
whose hands reach into the ground and sprout,
to him the soil is a divine drug. He enters into death
yearly, and comes back rejoicing. He has seen the light lie down
in the dung heap, and rise again in the corn.
His thought passes along the row ends like a mole.
What miraculous seed has he swallowed
that the unending sentence of his love flows out of his mouth
like a vine clinging in the sunlight, and like water
descending in the dark?

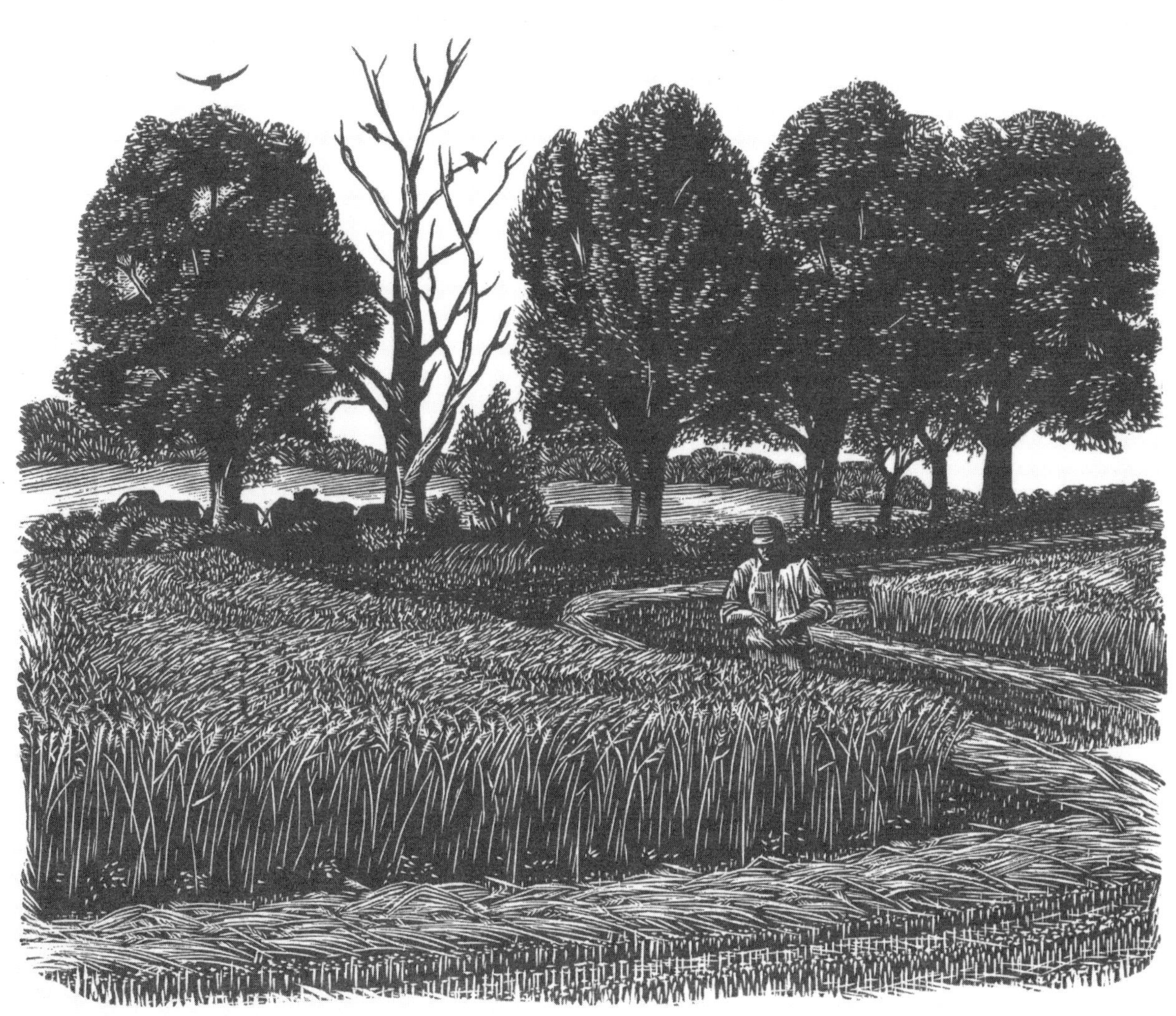

THE BUILDINGS

The buildings are all womanly. Their roofs
are like the flanks of mares, the arms and the hair of wives.
The future prepares its satisfaction in them.
In their dark heat I labor all summer, making them ready.
A time of death is coming, and they desire to live.
It is only the labor surrounding them that is manly,
the seasonal bringing in from the womanly fields
to the womanly enclosures. The house too yearns for life,
and hot paths come to it out of the garden and the fields,
full of the sun and weary. The wifeliness of my wife
is its welcome, a vine with yellow flowers shading the door.

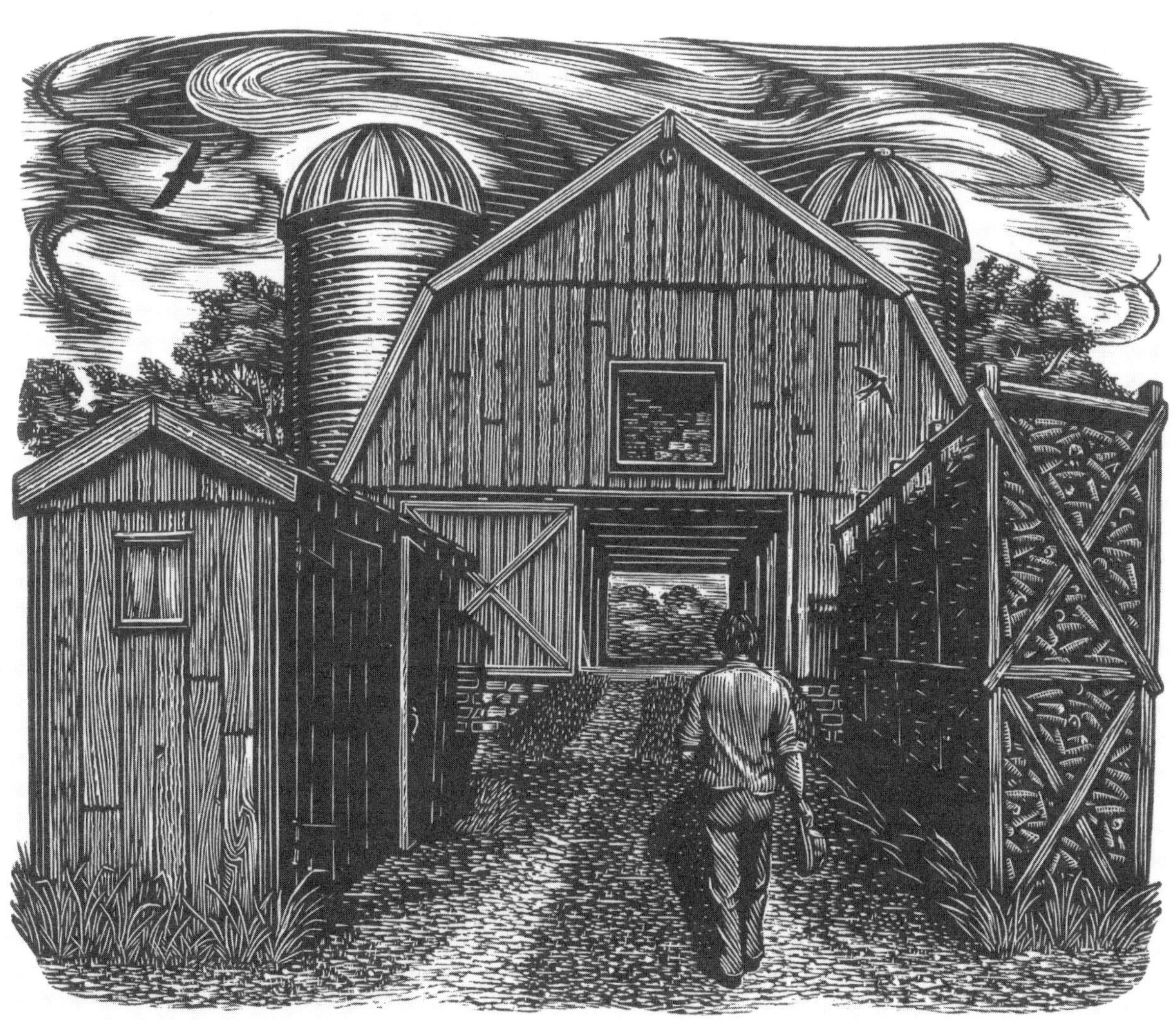

THE SEEDS

The seeds begin abstract as their species,
remote as the name on the sack
they are carried home in: Fayette Seed Company
Corner of Vine and Rose. But the sower
going forth to sow sets foot
into time to come, the seeds falling
on his own place. He has prepared a way
for his life to come to him, if it will.
Like a tree, he has given roots
to the earth, and stands free.

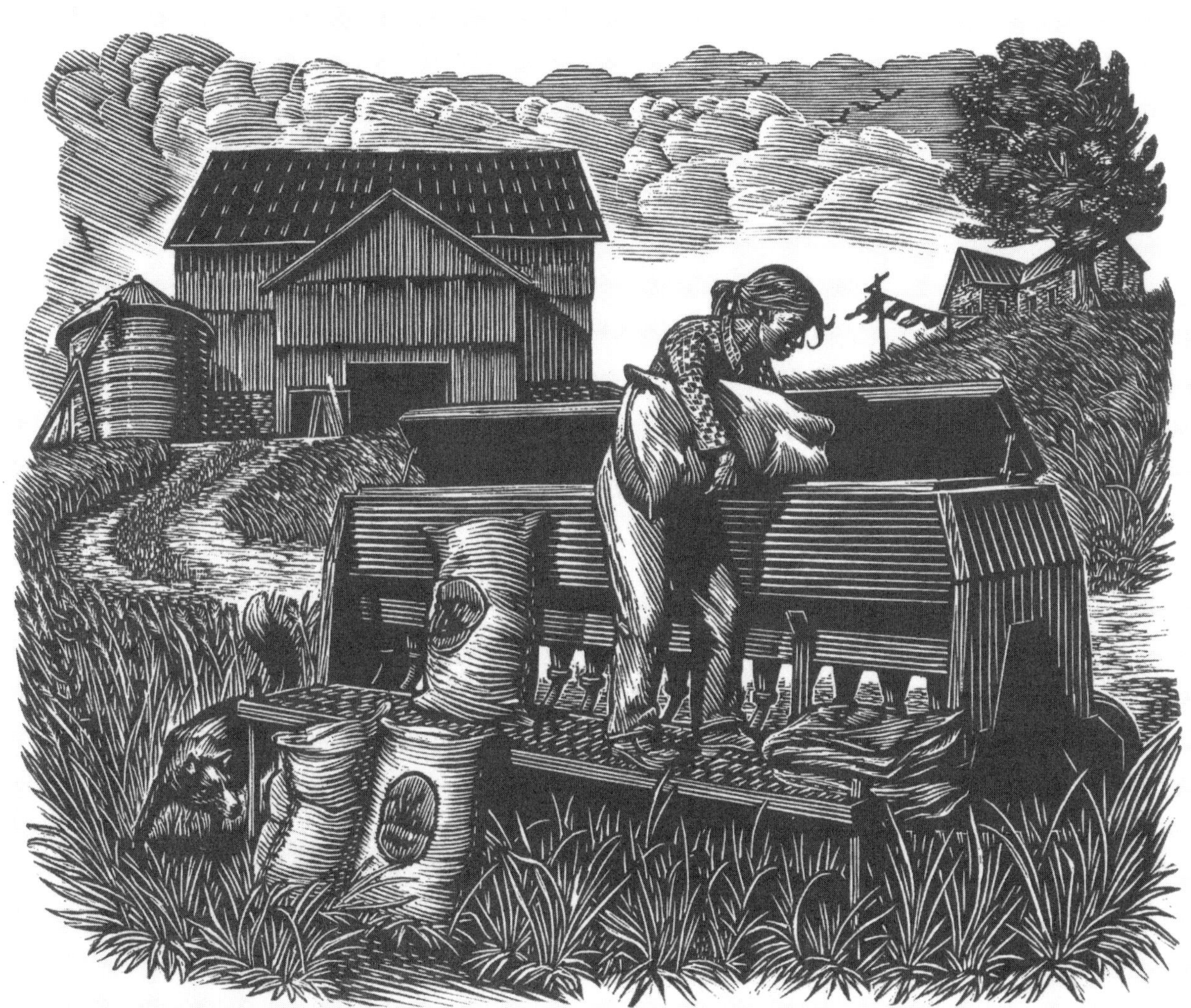

THE CURRENT

Having once put his hand into the ground,
seeding there what he hopes will outlast him,
a man has made a marriage with his place,
and if he leaves it his flesh will ache to go back.
His hand has given up its birdlife in the air.
It has reached into the dark like a root
and begun to wake, quick and mortal, in timelessness,
a flickering sap coursing upward into his head
so that he sees the old tribespeople bend
in the sun, digging with sticks, the forest opening
to receive their hills of corn, squash, and beans,
their lodges and graves, and closing again.
He is made their descendant, what they left
in the earth rising into him like a seasonal juice.
And he sees the bearers of his own blood arriving,
the forest burrowing into the earth as they come,
their hands gathering the stones up into walls,
and relaxing, the stones crawling back into the ground
to lie still under the black wheels of machines.
The current flowing to him through the earth
flows past him, and he sees one descended from him,
a young man who has reached into the ground,
his hand held in the dark as by a hand.

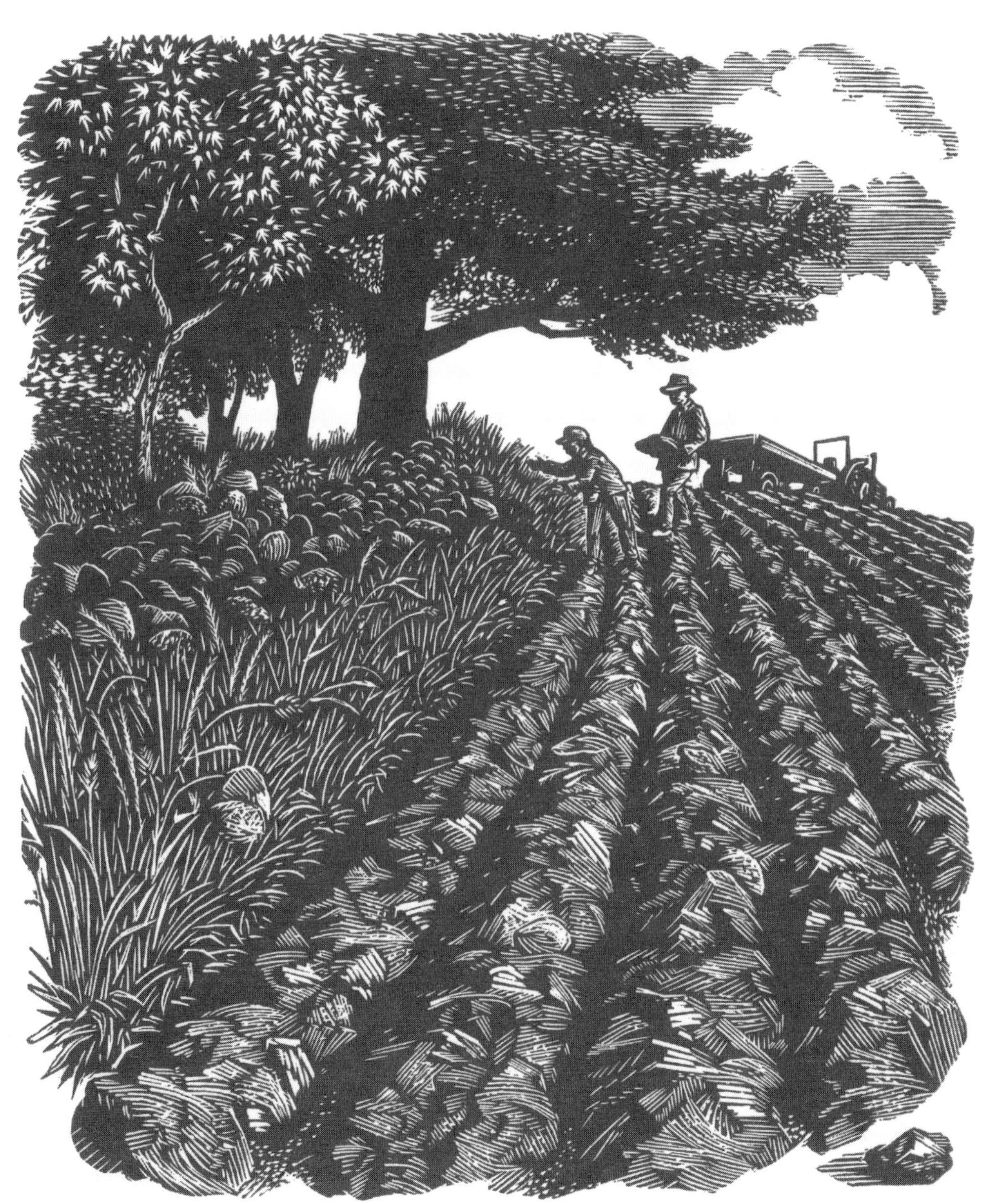

THE BARN

While we unloaded the hay from the truck, building
the great somnolence of the ricked bales, the weather
kept up its movement over us, the rain dashed and drove
against the roof, and in the close heat we sweated
to the end of the load. The fresh warm sweet smell
of new timothy in it, the barn is a nut ripened
in forethought of cold. Weighted now, it turns
toward the future generously, spacious
in its intent, the fledged young of the barn swallows
fluttering on the rim of the nest, the brown bats
hanging asleep, folded, beneath the rafters.
And we rest, having done what men are best at.

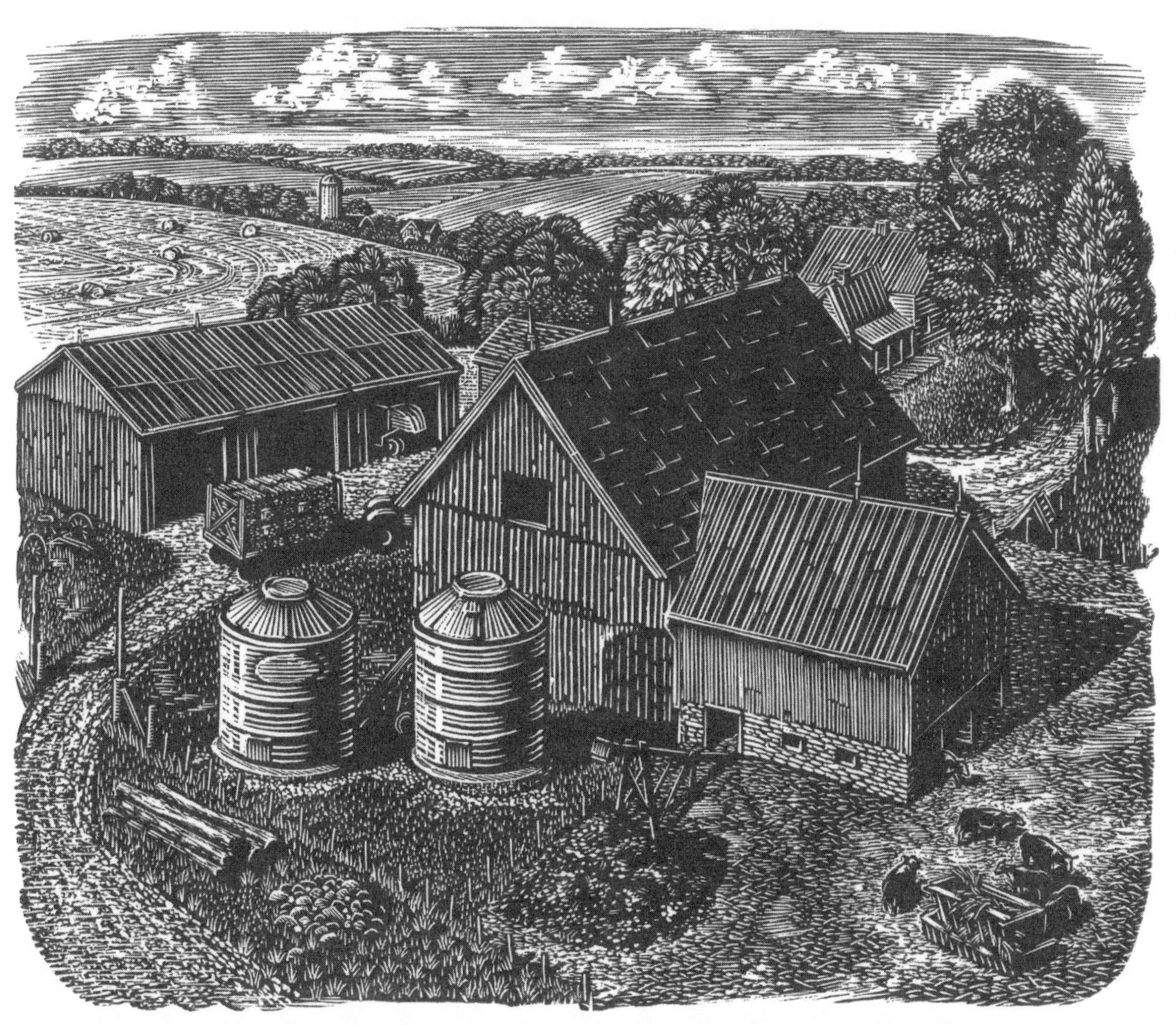

THE FARMER, SPEAKING OF MONUMENTS

Always, on their generation's breaking wave,
men think to be immortal in the world,
as though to leap from water and stand
in air were simple for a man. But the farmer
knows no work or act of his can keep him
here. He remains in what he serves
by vanishing in it, becoming what he never was.
He will not be immortal in words.
All his sentences serve an art of the commonplace,
to open the body of a woman or a field
to take him in. His words all turn
to leaves, answering the sun with mute
quick reflections. Leaving their seed, his hands
have had a million graves, from which wonders
rose, bearing him no likeness. At summer's
height he is surrounded by green, his
doing, standing for him, awake and orderly.
In autumn, all his monuments fall.

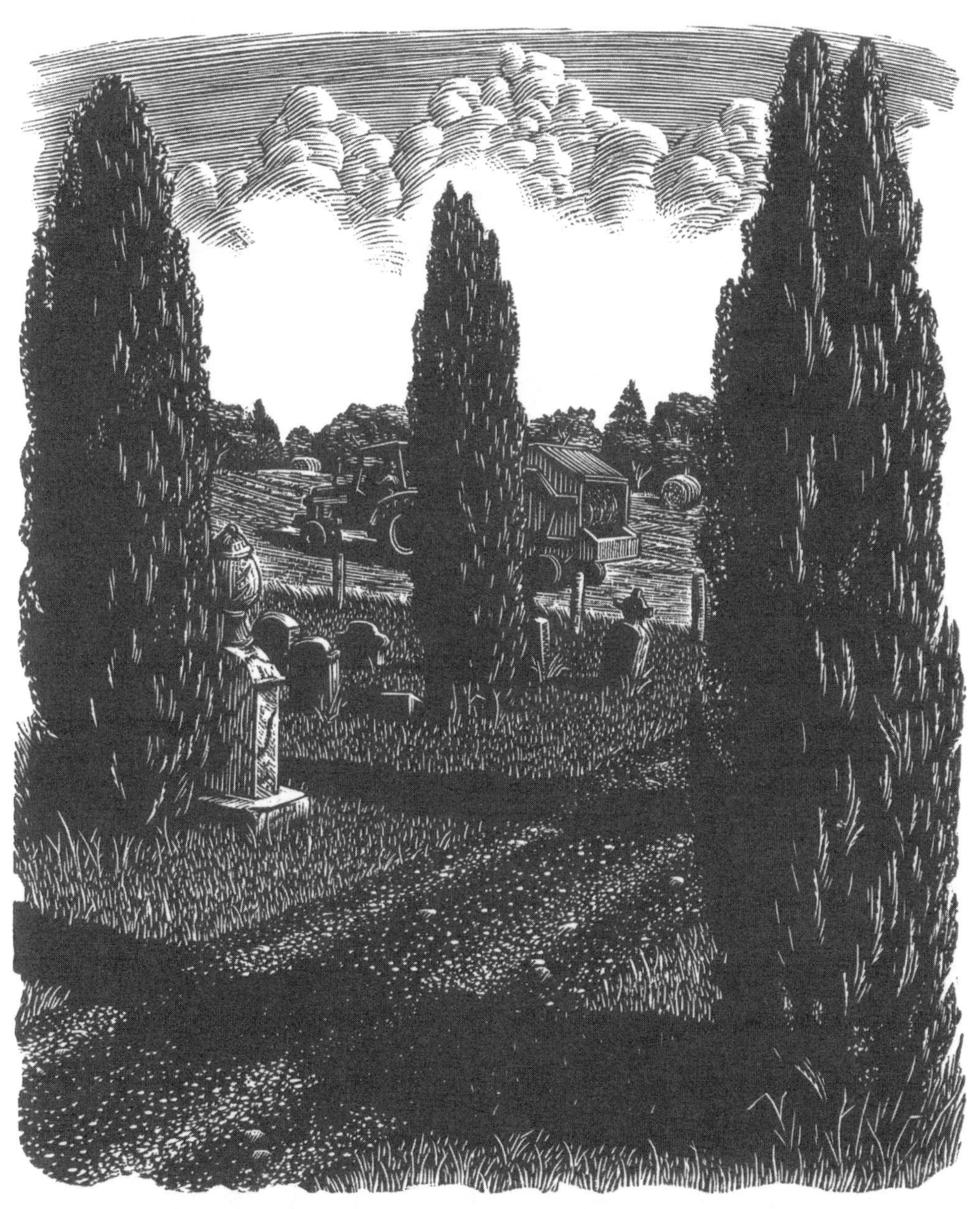

THE FEARFULNESS OF HANDS THAT HAVE LEARNED KILLING

The fearfulness of hands that have learned killing
I inherit from my own life. With my hands from boyhood
I formed the small perfect movements of death,
killing for pleasure or wantonness, casually.
Manhood taught me the formal deadliness
of hunter and farmer, the shedding
of predestined blood that lives for death.
Only marrying and fathering lives
has taught me the depth of ruin,
and made me feel quick in my hands the subtlety
and warmth of what they have destroyed.
And still I have killed for pity, and felt open
in my mind the beautiful silence, the sudden
ridding of a hurt thing's pain. I
am dumbfounded at the works I have accomplished
at the bounds of mystery, seeing it flow out
red and mute, matting the hair of my hands.
The skill that is prepared in me is careful
and terrible. There is no life I can think of
without sensing in my hands the answering power.
I shall not go free of the art of death.

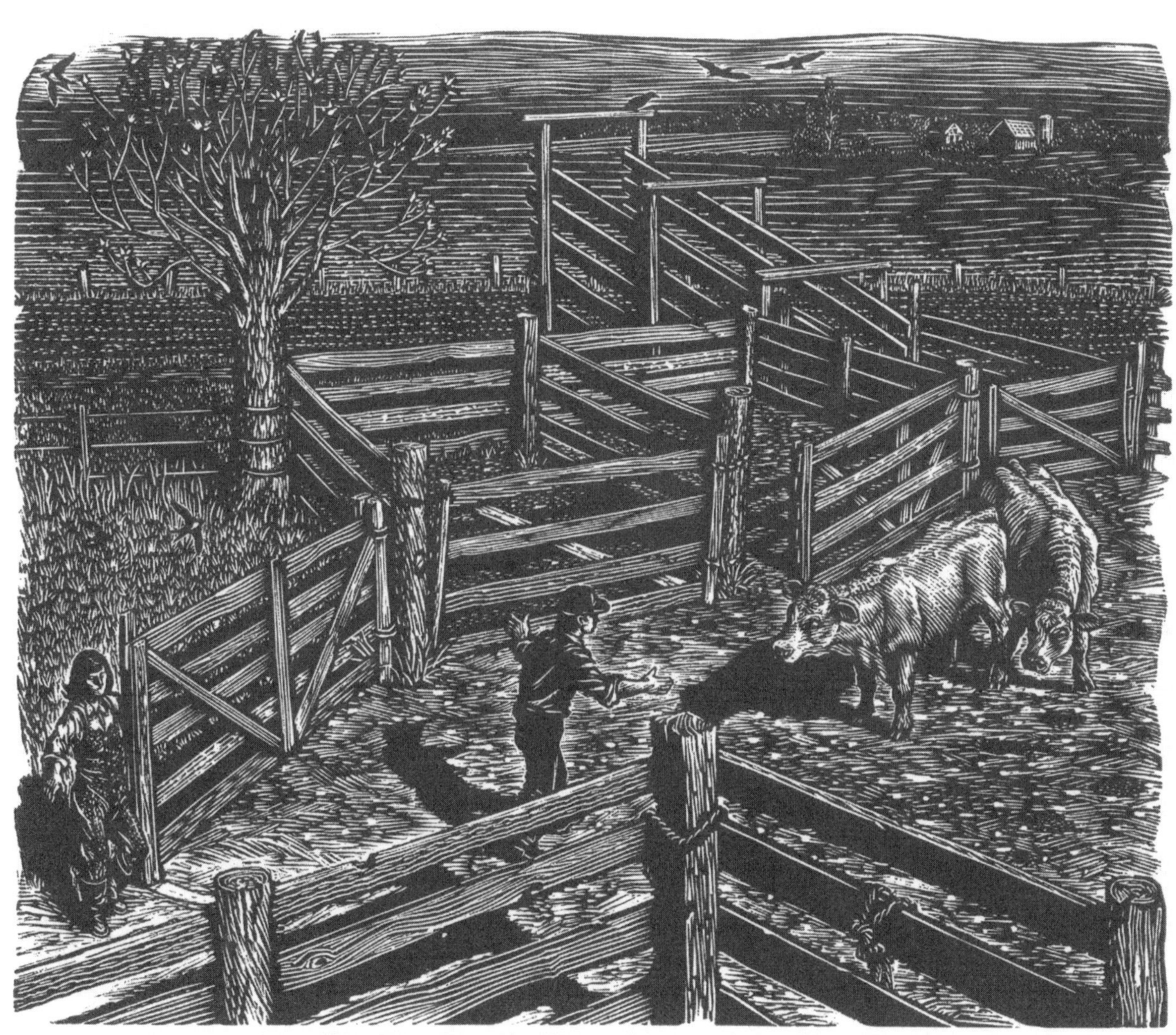

ENRICHING THE EARTH

To enrich the earth I have sowed clover and grass
to grow and die. I have plowed in the seeds
of winter grains and of various legumes,
their growth to be plowed in to enrich the earth.
I have stirred into the ground the offal
and the decay of the growth of past seasons
and so mended the earth and made its yield increase.
All this serves the dark. Against the shadow
of veiled possibility my workdays stand
in a most asking light. I am slowly falling
into the fund of things. And yet to serve the earth,
not knowing what I serve, gives a wideness
and a delight to the air, and my days
do not wholly pass. It is the mind's service,
for when the will fails so do the hands
and one lives at the expense of life.
After death, willing or not, the body serves,
entering the earth. And so what was heaviest
and most mute is at last raised up into song.

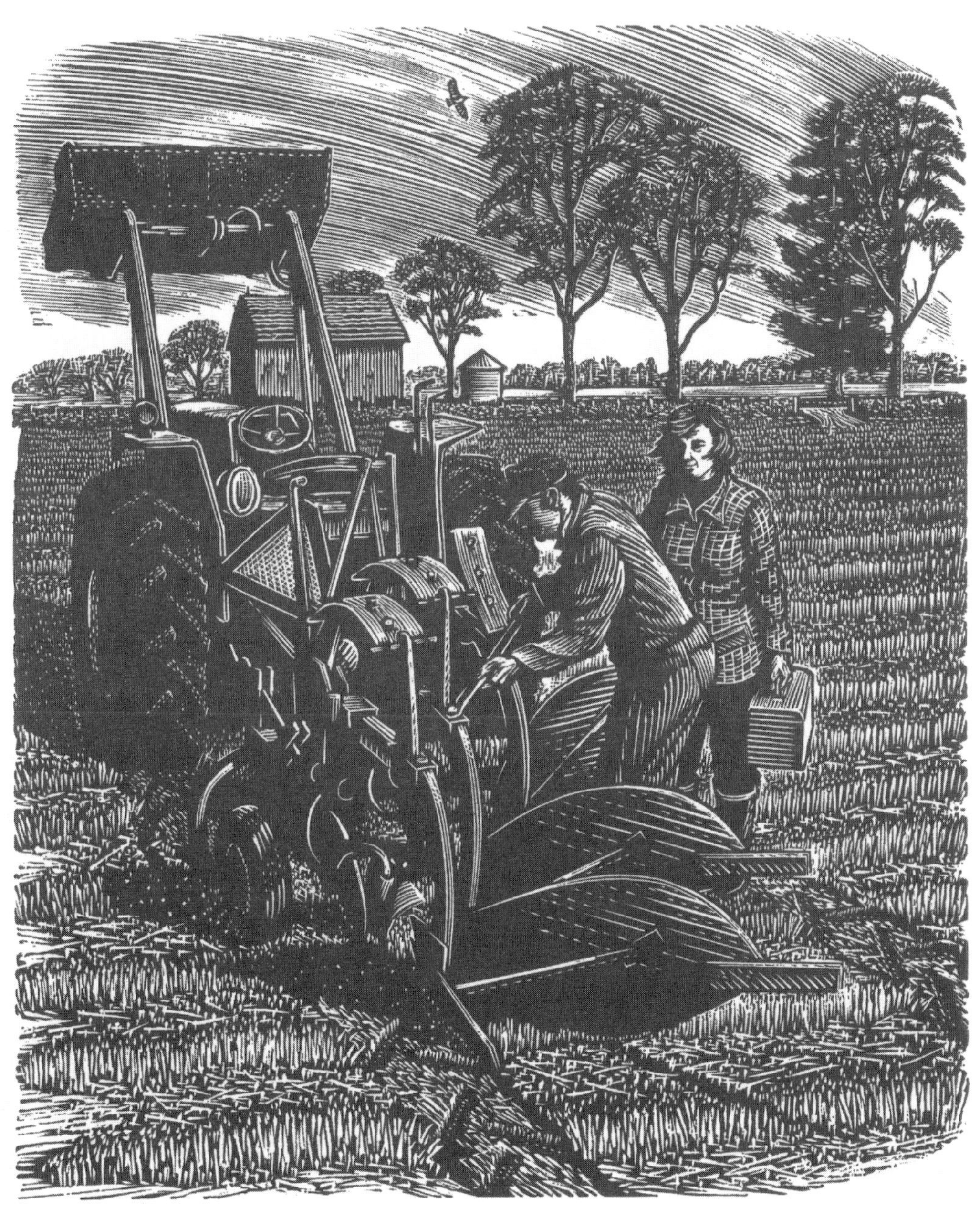

THE BRANCH WAY OF DOING

Danny Branch is older than Andy Catlett by about two years, which matter to them far less now than when they were young. They are growing old together with many of the same things in mind, many of the same memories. They often are at work together, just the two of them, taking a kind of solace and an ordinary happiness from their profound knowledge by now of each other's ways and of how to do whatever they are doing. They don't talk much. There is little to explain, they both are likely to know the same news, and Danny anyhow, unlike his father, rarely has anything extra to say.

Andy has always known Danny, but he knows that, to somebody who has not long known him, Danny might be something of a surprise. As if by nature, starting with the circumstances of his birth, as if by his birth he had been singled out and set aside, he has never been a conventional man. To Andy he has been not only a much-needed friend, but also, along with Lyda and their children, a subject of enduring interest and of study.

Danny is the son of Kate Helen Branch and Burley Coulter. His family situation was never formalized by a wedding between his parents, who for various and changing reasons lived apart, but were otherwise as loving and faithful until death as if bound by vows. And Danny was as freely owned and acknowledged, and about as attentively cared for and instructed, by Burley as by Kate Helen. 'He's my boy,' Burley would say to anybody who may have wondered. 'He was caught in my trap.'

And so Danny grew up, learning by absorption the frugal, elaborate housekeeping of his mother through the Depression and afterward, and grew up also, from the time he could walk, in the tracks of his father which led to work, to the woods, to the river, sometimes to town. Danny learned as they went along what came from work, what came, more freely, from the river and the woods, what came even from the easy, humorous talk of his father and his friends.

The whole story of Burley Coulter will never be known, let alone told. Maybe more than his son, he would have been a surprise to somebody expecting the modern version of homo sapiens. He loved the talk and laughter of work crews and the loafing places of Port William, but he was known also to disappear from such gatherings to go hunting or fishing alone, sometimes not to be seen by anybody for two or three days. Everybody knew, from testimony here and there, from gossip, that he had been by nature and almost from boyhood a ladies' man. Little girls had dreamed they would grow up and marry him, and evidently a good many bigger girls had had the same idea. But he remained a free man until, as he put it, Kate Helen had put a bit in his mouth and reined him up. But nobody had heard much more than that from Burley himself. He was full of stories, mostly funny, mostly at his own expense, but they never satisfied anybody's curiosity about his love life. He never spoke disrespectfully of a woman. He never spoke of intimacy with a woman. And so Port William speculated and imagined and labored over what it believed to be his story, receiving the testimony of many of its own authorities: 'Why, he did! I know damn well he did!' And Burley quietly amused himself by offering no help at all. It is possible, Andy thinks, that Burley was the hero of a work of fiction, of which he was hardly innocent, but a work of fiction nevertheless, composed entirely in the conversation of Port William.

Burley knew the way questions followed him, and he enjoyed the chase, preserving himself unto himself sometimes, like a well-running red fox, by arts of evasion, sometimes by artful semi-truths. Those who thought to catch him were most apt to catch a glimpse as he fled or perhaps flew, a mere shadow on the horizon. When he stood and faced you, therefore, as he did stand and face the people he loved, his candor would be felt as a gift given. But in ordinary conversation with the loafers and bystanders of Port William, he could be elusive.

'Where was you at last night, Burley? I come over to see you, and you wasn't home.'

'I stepped out a while.'

'Well, I reckon your dogs must've stepped out too. I didn't see no dogs.'

'My dogs do step out.'

'Reckon you all was stepping out off up Katy's Branch somewhere?'

'A piece farther, I reckon.'

'Well, now, where?'

'Well, till full day I didn't altogether exactly know.'

'If I couldn't hunt and know where I was, damned if I wouldn't stay home.'

'Oh, I knew where I was, but I didn't know where where I was was.'

Danny, his father's son and heir in many ways, always has been a more domestic man, and a quieter one, than his father. In 1950, two years after the law allowed him to quit school and he started farming 'full time' for himself, he married Lyda, and the two of them moved in with Burley, who had been living in the old house on the Coulter home place alone ever since his mother died.

For seven years Danny and Lyda had no children, and then in the following ten years they had seven: Will, Royal, Coulter, Fount, Reuben, and finally *('Finally!'* Lyda said) the two girls, Rachel and Rosie. Lyda, who had been Lyda Royal, had grown up in a family of ten children, and she said that the Lord had put her in this world to have some more. Like Danny, she had grown up poor and frugal. 'If my daddy shot a hawk that was killing our hens, we ate the hawk.'

She was about as tall as Danny, stoutly framed but not fat, a woman of forthright strength and presence whose unwavering countenance made it easy to remember that she was blue-eyed. She and Danny are the best-matched couple, Andy thinks, that he has ever known. That they had picked each other out and become a couple when they were hardly more than children and married before they could vote seems

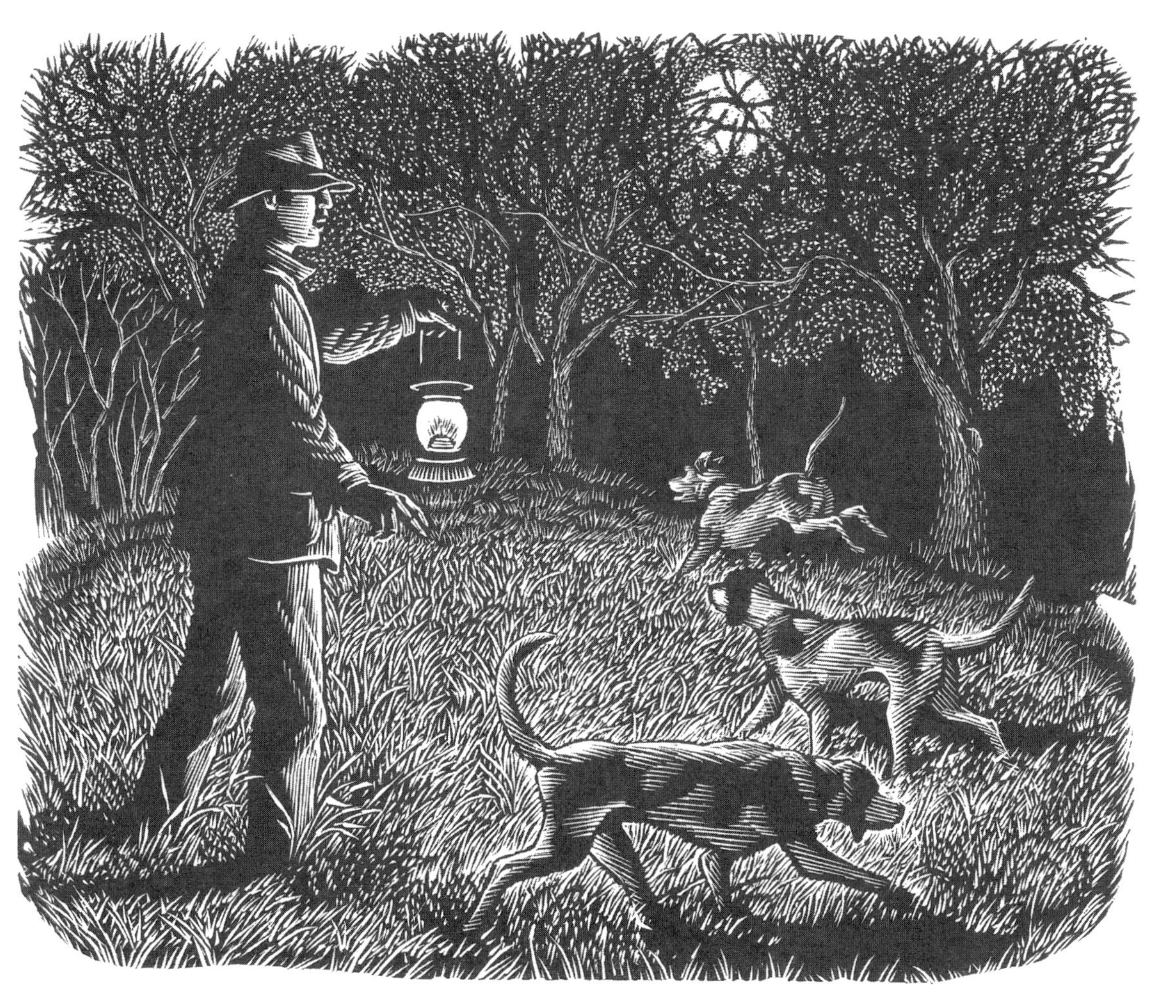

to Andy nothing less than a wonder. He supposes that they must have had, both of them, the gift of precocious self-knowledge, which could only have seemed wondrous to Andy, whose own mind has come clear to him slowly and at the cost of much labor.

For a further wonder, Danny and Lyda seem to have understood from the start that they would have to make a life together that would be determinedly marginal to the modern world and its economy—a realization that only began to come to Andy with the purchase of the Harford place when he was thirty. It was already present in Danny's mind at the age of sixteen, when nearly everybody around Port William was buying a tractor, and he stuck with his team of mules.

Marginality, conscious and deliberate, *principled* marginality, as Andy eventually realized, was an economic practice, informed by something like a moral code, and ultimately something like religion. No Branch of Danny's line ever spoke directly of morality or religion, but their practice, surely for complex reasons, was coherent enough that their ways were known in the Port William neighborhood and beyond by the name of Branch. 'That's a Branch way of doing,' people would say. Or by way of accusation: 'You trying to be some kind of Branch?'

To such judgments—never entirely condemnatory, but leaning rather to caution or doubt or bewilderment, for there was a lot of conventional advice that the Branches did not take—it became almost conventional to add, 'They're a good-*looking* family of people.' The good looks of Danny and Lyda when they were a young couple became legendary among those who remembered them as they were then. Their children were good-looking—'Of course,' people said—and moreover they looked pretty much alike. Danny and Lyda were a good cross.

Their economic life, anyhow, has been coherent enough to have kept the Branch family coherent. By 2004, Branch children and grandchildren are scattered through the Port William neighborhood, as Lyda says, like the sage in sausage. They stick together—whether for fear of Lyda, or because they like each other, or just because they are alike, is a question often asked but never settled. Wherever you find a Branch household you are going to find a lot of food being raised, first to eat and then to sell or give away, also a lot of free provender from the waters and the woods. You are going to find a team, at least, of horses or mules. But there are Branches catering to the demand for heavy pulling horses. Some keep brood mares and sell anything from weanlings to broke farm teams. If a team will work cheaper or better than a tractor, a Branch will use a team. But with a few exceptions in the third generation, they also can fix anything mechanical, and so no Branch has ever owned a new car or truck or farm implement. Their habit is to find something that nobody else wants, or that everybody else has given up on, and then tow or haul it home, fix it, and use it.

As they live at the margin of the industrial economy, they live also at the margin of the land economy. They can't afford even moderately good land, can't even think of it. And so such farms as they have managed to own are small, no better than the steep-sided old Coulter place where Danny and Lyda have lived their married life, no better even than the much abused and neglected Riley Harford place that Andy and Flora Catlett had bought in 1964.

The Branch family collectively is an asset to each of its households, and often to their neighbors as well. This may be the surest and the best of the reasons for their success, which is to say their persistence and their modest thriving. When the federal tobacco program finally was defeated, and with it the tobacco economy of the small farmers, and when, with that, the the long tradition of work-swapping among neighbors, even acquaintance with neighbors, was petering out, the Branches continued to swap work. They helped each other. When they knew their neighbors needed help, they went and helped their neighbors. If you bought something the Branches had for sale, and they were always likely to have something to sell, or if

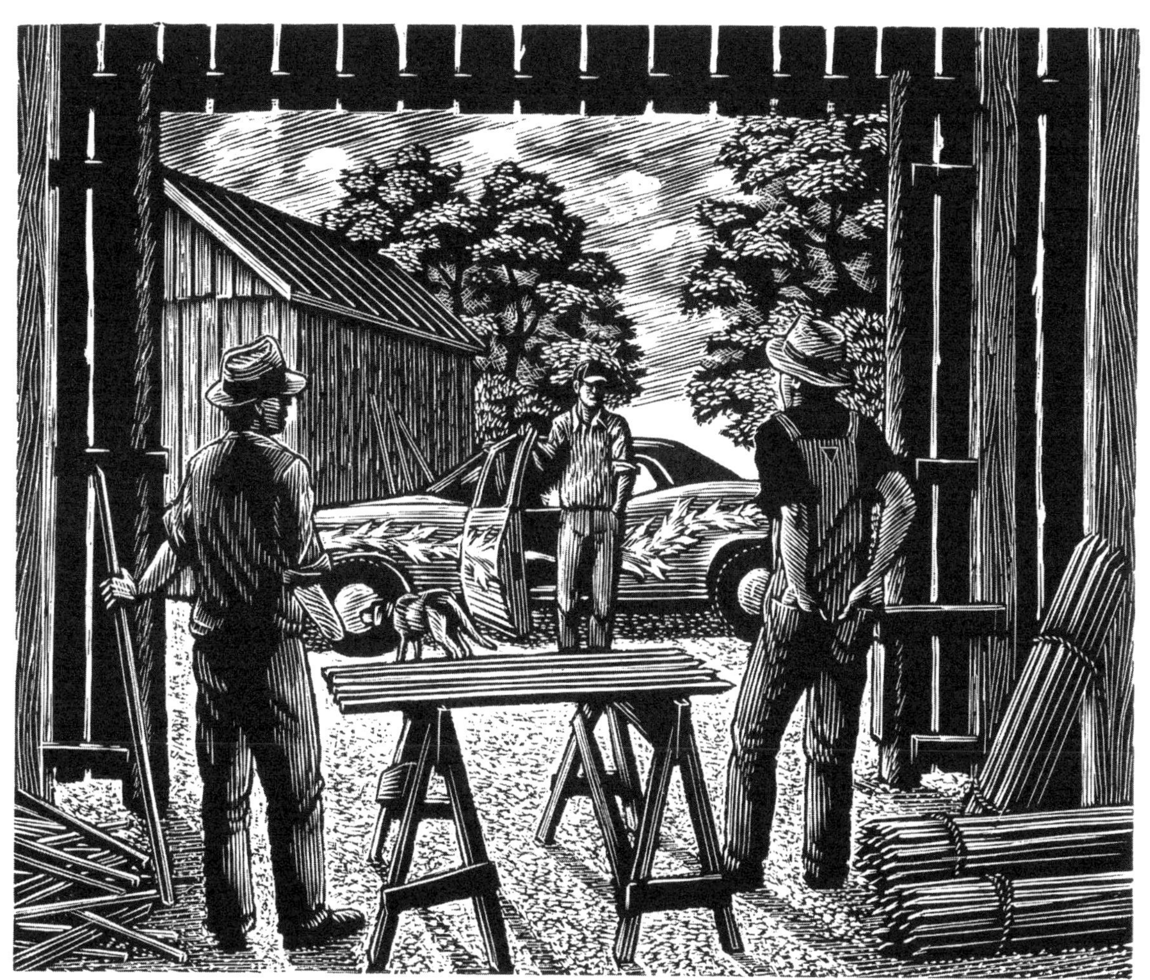

you hired them, they expected of course to be paid. If, on the contrary, they went to help a neighbor in need, they considered their help a gift, and so they would accept no pay. These transactions would end with a bit of conversation almost invariable, almost a ritual:

'Well, what I owe you?'

'Aw, I'm liable to need help myself sometime.'

The old neighborly ways of Port William, dying out rapidly at the start of the third millennium, have survived in Danny and Lyda Branch, and have been passed on to their children. The one boast that Andy ever heard from Danny was that he had worked on all his neighbors' farms and had never taken a cent of money in payment. After his boys grew big enough to work, and he knew of a neighbor in need of help, instead of going himself he would sometimes send a couple of the boys. He would tell them: 'If they offer you dinner, you can eat, but don't you come back here with any money.'

This uneasiness about money Andy recognizes from much else that he has known of the people of Port William and similar places. Free exchanges of work and other goods they managed easily, but transactions of money among friends and neighbors nearly always involved an embarrassment that they had to alleviate by much delay, much conversation, as if to make the actual handing of cash or a check incidental to a social occasion. It was not, Andy thought, that they agreed with the scripture that 'the love of money is the root of all evil,' but that from a time even older they held a certain distrust against money itself, or the idea of it, as if a *token* of value were obviously inferior to, obviously worse than, a *thing* of value. And so a man, understanding himself as a neighbor, could not accept money as in any way representative of work or goods given in response to a need.

The Branches, then, would have things to sell. They would work now and then for wages. At convenience or if they had to, they would spend. But their aim, as often as possible, was to have a choice: something they could do or make or find instead of spending money, even of earning it.

Of the source and the reasons for this Branch fastidiousness, Andy is still unsure. For himself, he has finally understood that, however it may be loved for itself, money is only symbolic, only the means of purchasing something that is not money. To live almost entirely, or entirely, by purchase, as many modern people do, is to equate the worth of every actual thing with its price. The symbol thus comes to limit and control the thing it symbolizes, and like a rust or canker finally consumes it. And so buying and selling for money is not simply a matter of numbers and accounting, but is a dark and fearful mystery.

Do the Branches know this? Because he so imperfectly knows it himself, Andy has not known how to ask Danny or Lyda if they know it. He knows only that they, and their children too, seem to be living from some profound motive of good will, even of good cheer, that shows itself mainly in their practice of their kind of economy. The Branches are not much given to explaining.

And so in addition to being included in their friendship, benefitting from it, knowing them well, and loving them in just return, Andy has studied them with endless liking and fascination, feeling always that there is yet more that he needs to know. He believes that the way they live, and the way they are, can be summed up, not explained, by a set of economic principles, things Danny could have told his children but probably never did, or needed to. Andy, anyhow, after many years of observing and pondering, has made a list of instructions that he hears in Danny's voice, whether or not Danny can be supposed ever to have said them:

1 Be happy with what you've got. Don't be always looking for something better.
2 Don't buy anything you don't need.
3 Don't buy what you ought to save. Don't buy what you ought to make.

4 Unless you absolutely have got to do it, don't buy anything new.
5 If somebody tries to sell you something to 'save labor,' look out. If you can work, then work.
6 If other people want to buy a lot of new stuff and fill up the country with junk, *use* the junk.
7 Some good things are cheap, even free. Use them first.
8 Keep watch for what nobody wants. Sort through the leavings.
9 You might know, or find out, what it is to need help. So help people.

Andy heard Danny say only one thing of this kind, but what he said summed up all the rest.

When he was just old enough to have a driver's license, Reuben, Danny and Lyda's youngest boy, raised a tobacco crop and spent almost all he earned from it on a car. It was a used car—Reuben, after all, was a Branch—but it was a fancy car. Lyda thought the car was intended to appeal to a certain girl. The girl, it turned out, was more impressed with another boy's car, so Reuben got only his car for his money, plus, as his mother told him soon enough, his good luck in losing the girl. Though all in vain, the car was bright red, and had orange and black flames painted on its sides, and had a muffler whose mellow tone announced that Reuben was more rank and ready than he actually was.

Andy and Danny were at work together in Andy's barn when Reuben arrived in his new-to-him car. He had promised his help, and he was late. He drove right up to the barn door, where his red and flaming vehicle could hardly have looked more unexpected. He gunned the engine, let it gargle to a stop, and got out. Maybe he had already had a second thought or two, for a touch of sheepishness was showing through his pride. Danny favored his son with a smile that Reuben was not able to look away from. Reuben had to stand there, smiling back, while, still smiling, his father looked him over. When Danny spoke he spoke in a tone of merriment—the epithet he used seemed almost indulgent—but his tone was nonetheless an emphasis upon a difference that he clearly regarded as fundamental: Some people work hard for what they have, and other people are glad to take it from them easily. What he said Andy has remembered ever since as a cry of freedom: 'Sweetheart, I told you. And you'll learn. Don't let the sons of bitches get ahold of your money.'

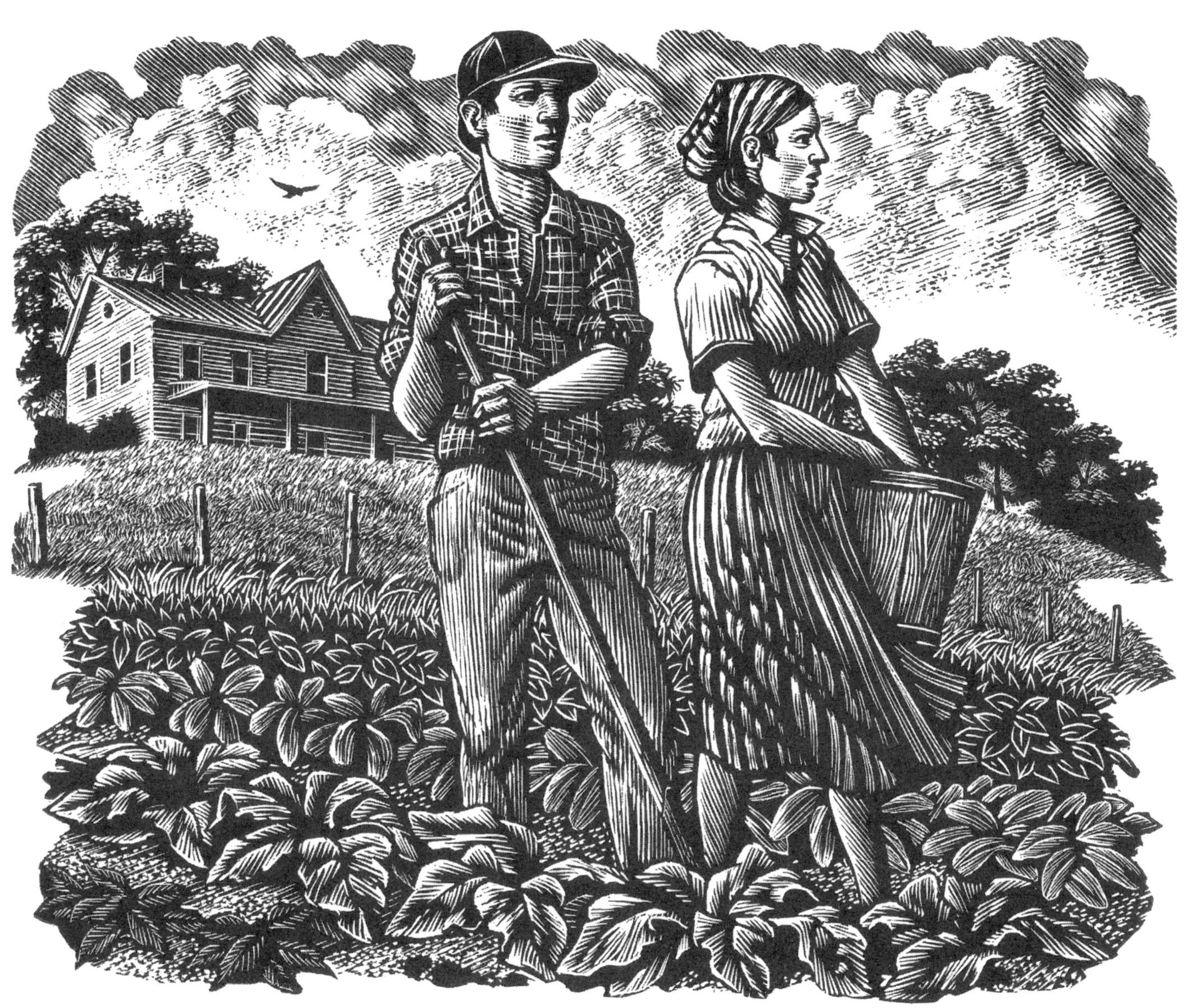

Wendell Berry is the author of more than fifty books of poetry, fiction and essays. He was awarded the National Humanities Medal by Barak Obama (2010) and in 2012 delivered the forty-first annual Jefferson Lecture in the Humanities, the highest honor the federal government has for distinguished intellectual achievement in the humanities. He lives and works with his wife, Tanya Berry, on their farm in Port Royal, Kentucky.

Wesley Bates is an acclaimed artist who is primarily known for his brilliant wood engravings, but also works in various other mediums. Bates was born in the Yukon Territory and for many years has had a studio in Ontario where he operates the West Meadow Press.

In 1995, Wendell Berry's *Roots to the Earth* was published in portfolio form by West Meadow Press. The wood etchings of celebrated artist and wood engraver, Wesley Bates, were printed from the original wood blocks on handmade Japanese paper.

In 2014, this work was reprinted along with additional poems. Together with Bates' original wood engravings, and designed by Gray Zeitz, Larkspur Press printed just one hundred copies of this book in a stunning limited edition.

Now it is with great pleasure that Counterpoint is reproducing this collaborative work for trade publication, as well as expanding it with the inclusion of the prize-winning never before published in book form short story, "The Branch Way of Doing," with additional engravings by Bates.

In his introduction to the 2014 collection, Bates wrote: "As our society moves toward urbanization, the majority of the population views agriculture from an increasingly detached position. . . . In his poetry [Berry] reveals tenderness and love as well as anger and uncertainty. . . . The wood engravings in this collection are intended to be companion pieces to . . . the way he expresses what it is to be a farmer."